MUSIC THEORY: FOR BEGINNERS

The Only 7 Exercises You Need to Learn Music Fundamentals and the Elements of Written Music Today

Preston Hoffman

Table of Contents

Introduction

Thank you and congratulations on purchasing this book, *"Music Theory: For Beginners"* I have written this book to provide you with the steps that you need to take to understand the fundamentals of music theory from a beginner's standpoint.

One of the most common problems that many people face when it comes to music theory is the inability to get a good book that sticks to the fundamental aspects. Music theory is not exactly a topic that will get your heart pounding, so most people want content that will explain music fundamentals in a clear and concise manner. Most music theory books either bore the reader with long, drawn-out explanations, or they toss in some complex concepts that leave you totally confused.

However, this is where this book is different. This book provides you with the only seven exercises that you need as a beginner to master the fundamental elements of written music. These interactive exercises are all based on seven topics that form the basis of every good music theory course. The exercises are spread throughout the book so that once you finish reading each chapter, you can test yourself. I have taken the time to make the questions as challenging as possible yet simple enough for any beginner to understand. In any case, the answers have been provided at the end of the book.

You will not find yourself struggling with complex theories here. I have written this book with the beginner in mind, so every chapter covers a single aspect of music theory. This is to ensure that you move step-by-step, mastering one foundational topic before you move onto the next one. You will learn the common notation system, scales, clefs, key signatures, intervals, chords, and much more.

I have tried to make sure that the topics move sequentially in terms of the level of difficulty. My goal is to take your hand and walk you through every topic and exercise so that you feel comfortable with the content. From my experience with reading and writing music, I know that if you get the first step right, then the next one will automatically fall into place.

By the time you finish reading this book, you will be much more confident in reading and even writing your own music. Yes, it's true! The exercises you will go through in this book will test you and help you grow your musical abilities. I can promise you that with this book, you will finally get to learn all you ever wanted to know about music theory in a fun and interactive way. This is a personal guarantee!

Are you ready? Let's go!

Chapter One: Understanding Music Theory

In this chapter, you will learn about what music theory is all about and why it is important for beginners to have a firm theoretical foundation. You will also go through a brief and painless history of written music. Finally, you will get to discover the seven exercises that are fundamental to the learning of music.

What is Music Theory?

The simplest way to define music theory is this: It is the language that enables you to read, understand, and play any kind of music that has been composed. Music theory is made up of rules and concepts that are designed to govern the way music is written and performed.

Another way to look at it is that music is a language that consists of many various parts. Each part is then divided into smaller sections. If you want to learn how to speak the whole language, you must start by learning the smaller sections first and how to combine them to form the larger parts. Then you must learn how to put together those large parts to communicate whatever message you have through that language.

We learn music theory so that we know how to put the elements together to compose music. That is music theory in a nutshell.

As a beginner, it is easy to fall into the trap of feeling overwhelmed when you hear the words "music theory," but there is really nothing to worry about. The critical thing to keep in mind when learning about music theory is that the music preceded the theory. The art of making musical sounds dates back thousands of years, and at that time, our ancestors didn't have any kind of theory to rely on. They just pounded on their drums and played it by ear. If you are already playing an instrument, then you most likely have a rough idea about music theory. The only issue is that you haven't learned the terms and technicalities yet.

Like I said before, music theory is a language that allows musicians to read and perform compositions the way the composer intended. However, it is important to also note that there are some musicians who are not able to read or write music, yet they can still make awesome melodies and sounds. There are some people who can hear and speak English but cannot read or write it. Therefore, some people view learning music theory as boring and unnecessary.

On the other hand, I believe that a student can progress much further in learning a new language by training himself/herself to read and write it. It is the same with music theory. If you want to master new techniques, gain more confidence, and perform new styles, you need to learn music theory.

Now let's go back a bit into history to unearth the beginnings of music theory.

Musical Beginnings

According to historians, complex musical instruments were already being used as far back as 7000 B.C. Archaeologists have found bone flutes that can still be used to create short performances for modern listeners to hear.

There are pictographs from 3500 B.C. that depict the ancient Egyptians playing clarinets, harps, and lyres. By the year 1500 B.C., the people in Northern Syria had modified the Egyptian harp and created the first ever two-stringed guitar. The instrument even had tuning pegs and a hollow soundboard for amplifying sounds.

So why am I telling you all this?

If you look at the history of ancient music, you will realize that distinct cultures spread out all over the world were able to create music with very similar tonal qualities. How was this possible? It is believed that certain patterns of musical notes just sound right while others do not. If this is the case, then music theory is simply the search for why and how certain notes sound right or wrong. To put it more plainly, music theory is important because it helps us understand *why* an object sounds a particular way and *how* we can reproduce that exact sound.

Ancient Greece is believed to be the origin of music theory. The Greeks even built schools that taught the science and philosophy of analysing music. It was Pythagoras who went as far as creating the 12-pitch octave scale that resembles the one we currently use today. Pythagoras achieved this using a device known as the Circle of Fifths, which you will learn about later in this book.

A lot of the musical theory you are about to learn is based on the works of the ancient Greeks. But unlike the Greek language, this book is much simpler to read and understand.

The Significance of Theory in Your Music

It is easy to think that making great music is as simple as sitting down, playing whatever note you want, going in any direction you see fit, and even stopping at any stage of the performance. That is often the view of most aspiring musicians who would love to play an instrument.

However, such kind of performances, if they do exist, would cause confusion and sound annoying to the listeners. Only those musicians who have thoroughly mastered how to stack notes and chords adjacent to each other can manage to perform a spontaneous jam that listeners would love. In other words, since music is a language that communicates a message, you must learn how to connect with your listeners at all times.

Learning musical theory can also inspire you a great deal, as you will soon find out after you finish reading this book. It is a tremendously great feeling when you discover that you can put together a chord progression and create an awesome song out of it. How would you feel if you could look at a piece of classical music and know that you can play it for the first time?

What about being confident enough to call up your friends and ask them to come over and jam with you? You wouldn't be able to do that without learning music theory since you need a way to communicate with other musicians. You use music theory to talk to one another as you play your various instruments.

The truth is that music theory will broaden your horizons as a musician. If you see yourself as a potential rock guitarist, you will be able to know which notes to play in which key. If it's classical music you are interested in, you will know how to sight-read and maintain a consistent beat. Music is fun but it also requires a prominent level of discipline. At the end of it all, it is worth it!

The Seven Fundamental Exercises

There are a lot of elements that you will have to learn to become an accomplished musician. Of course, we all wish that we could somehow sit down with an instrument and start playing beautiful music without going through the hassle of any formal training. But the reality is that you need structured exercises that will prepare you for your future as a music maestro.

In the next few chapters, we are going to cover music theory fundamentals that will help you get started. There are seven elements that you will have to master to learn these elements effectively. They are:

1. Learning the staff and music alphabet

2. Common notation

3. Basic elements of music (rhythm, melody, harmony, etc)

4. Mastering the scales

5. Building intervals

6. Understanding key signatures

7. Forming chords

Every single one of these elements is critical to your progress as a beginner. They will teach you the individual elements of music and how they are put together to create a solid foundation for reading, playing, and studying music.

Chapter Summary

Here is a summary of the key points of this chapter:

- Music theory is the rules and concepts that enable us to read, understand, and play any kind of musical composition.
- It is possible to play music without learning music theory, but if you want to go further in learning new techniques and performing new styles, you must learn music theory.
- Though complex musical instruments date back as far as 7000 B.C., the ancient Greeks are the ones credited with establishing schools for analysing the elements of music.
- Learning musical theory will enable you to communicate more effectively with listeners and fellow musicians, while also inspiring confidence in your own musical abilities.
- There are seven key exercises that will help you learn the fundamentals of music theory.

In the next chapter, you will learn about the staff and how we use the music alphabet to write music. It isn't a difficult topic, but since the rest of the book will be based on what you learn in the next chapter, you need to make sure that you go through it thoroughly.

Chapter Two: Learning the Staff

In this chapter, you will learn about the staff. It is important to start by learning the main way that we write music. You will learn what the staff looks like, the several types of clefs, and how to arrange notes when writing your music. There will also an exercise at the end of the chapter to test what you have learned.

Human beings started making music way before writing was invented. Even to this day, some musicians choose to play "by ear," which means they don't rely on written music. However, it is important to write music so that it can be shared and studied. This means that we must have system to represent music, hence the need for a music alphabet.

What is the Music Alphabet?

The musical alphabet is an arrangement of letters that enables us to write the sounds that we want to play. Every time you sit down to play music with others, the first thing you do is talk about what you plan on playing. By talking I don't mean just telling each other stories or describing your music verbally. The language of communication should be specific to music, and that is where the music alphabet comes in. The alphabet is the means of representing your music.

Before we go into the musical notes themselves, let's start by learning about the most widespread way of writing music. This is the staff.

The Staff

Now that you have learned about the music alphabet, it's time to tackle a very important component of music. All instruments that play specific pitches are written on the staff, which is comprised of five horizontal parallel lines. Music notes are usually placed either on the lines or in the spaces between the lines. The music on a staff is read from left to right.

In the image below, you will notice some short lines that are above or below the staff. These are known as *ledger lines*. These are used to show a note that is too low or too high to be placed on the staff.

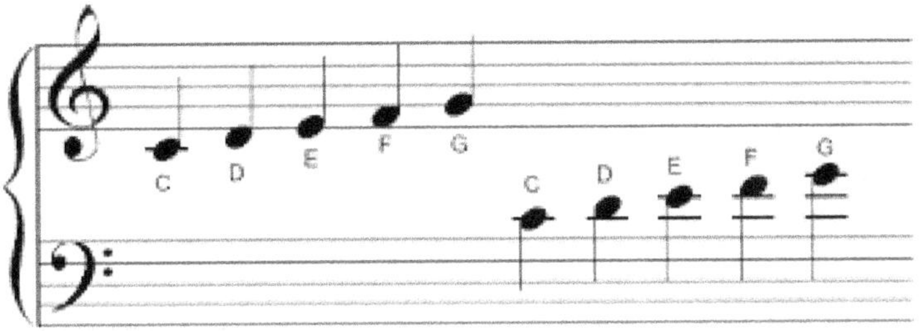

Figure 2.1

To make reading music much easier, vertical lines are used to split the staff into sections. These lines are known as **bar lines**. Each section that is formed on the staff is then called a **measure** or **bar**. At the end of every staff, there are two lines that mark the end of a section of music or song. These are known as **double bar lines**. A heavy double bar line indicates that you have reached the end of the song. A light double bar line means the end of a section of music.

Figure 2.2

You may be wondering what some of the symbols and shapes are on the staff above. These will be discussed later in this chapter.

Clefs

In figure 2.2, you notice a symbol that is placed at the beginning of the staff. This is the ***Clef symbol***. It tells you the type of note that is found on every line and space of the staff. There are two kinds of clefs; the treble clef (or G clef) and the bass clef (or F clef).

The reason why it's called a G clef is that its body curls around the line that represents the G note. For the F clef, the symbol curls around the line representing the F note. The notes in the staff are always arranged in ascending order from top to bottom, but they are positioned differently depending on the type of clef being used. The reason why we use different clefs is to cover as many notes within the human voice range as possible, as well as most of the instruments used. People and instruments with high voice ranges use the treble clef while those with lower ranges use bass clef.

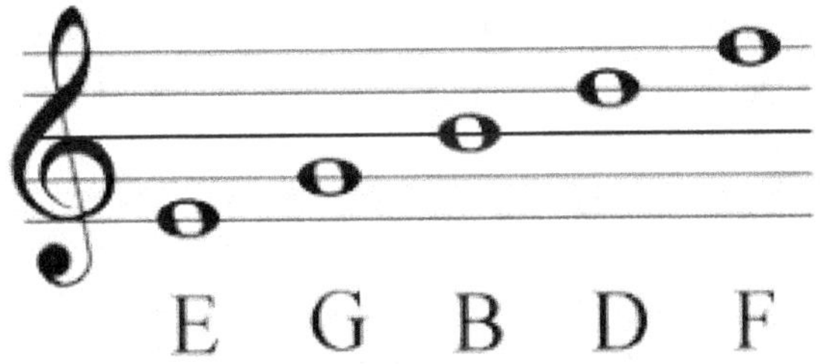

Figure 2.3

Figure 2.4

Exercise 1

1. Draw the staff on a piece of paper and practice writing the two clef symbols on the staff. Draw as many as you can until you learn it perfectly.

2. Draw the staff with treble and name all the spaces on the staff.

3. Draw the staff with bass clef and name the lines in it.

4. On a staff with a treble clef, name the ledger lines and spaces above the staff.

5. On a staff with a bass clef, name the lines and spaces below the staff.

Chapter Summary

Here are some key points you need to remember:

- The musical alphabet is an arrangement of letters that enable us to write the sounds that we want to play.
- The notes on the staff are placed either on the lines or in the spaces between the lines.
- Notes on the staff are arranged in ascending order.
- Ledger lines are used when showing notes that are too high or too low to appear on the staff.
- A bar line splits the staff into sections called measures or bars.
- A heavy double bar line indicates the end of a song.
- A light double bar line indicates the end of a section of music.

- There are two types of clef symbols – the treble clef and the bass clef.

In the next chapter, you will learn about music notation. These are considered the building blocks of music and are necessary when writing your music.

Chapter Three: Understanding Common Notation

In this chapter, you will learn the A-B-C's of the musical language. We will talk about the building blocks that form the foundation of musical theory. These include notes, pitch, octave, beats, and time signature. There will also an exercise at the end of the chapter to test what you have learned.

Common notation simply refers to the standard system that we use to represent music notes. It is more widely used than other types of music notation that have been invented, for example, tablature. You have already learned about one part of common notation in the previous chapter. Now let's talk about notes and pitches.

Notes

Every piece of music you will encounter consists of notes. They are the building blocks of music. A note is simply a letter of the musical alphabet that represents the *pitch* made by a musical instrument.

The pitch of a note refers to how low or high it sounds. Pitch is dependent on the frequency and wavelength of the sound wave of a note. If the frequency of the sound wave is high, and the wavelength is short, the pitch will be high. Since very few musicians are keen on such kind of physics terminologies, they use letters to represent different pitches.

There are seven letters that form the music alphabet. These are:

A B C D E F G A

or:

C D E F G A B C

These seven letters are used to name the white keys on a keyboard. As you can see above, you start with the letter A and proceed to the letter G. After G, instead of going to H, we go back and start counting from A. In music, each set of seven letters (A – G or C - B) is referred to as an *octave*. The moment you reach the eighth note, you begin the next octave.

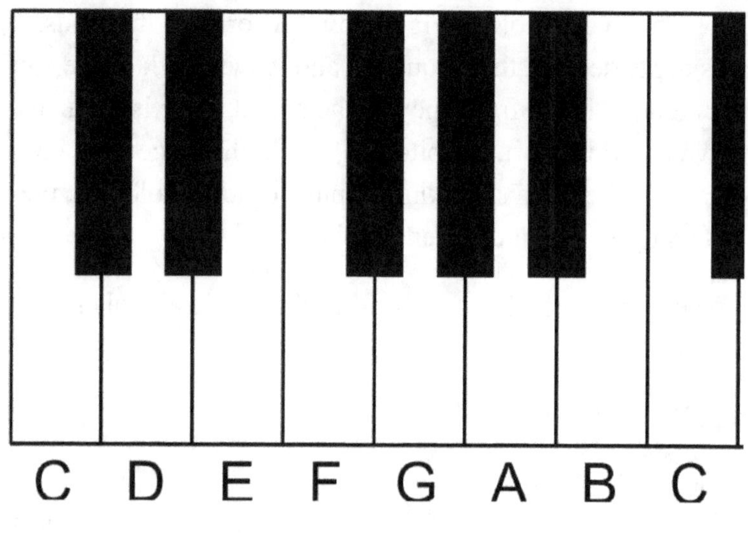

Figure 3.1

But there's one thing that you need to be keenly aware of here. As you move toward the right side, or *up the alphabet*, you realize that you will meet a note with the same letter name as another one before. However, this next note will be at a higher octave than the previous one.

In figure 3.1 above, the second C note has a pitch that is at a higher octave than the first. If you were to move up the alphabet, the third C note would be a higher pitch than the second one, and so on. You can also move in the opposite direction, and this is referred to as going *down the alphabet*.

Sharps and Flats

Though there are only seven letters in the music alphabet, there are more than seven notes. The seven letters from A to G represent *natural* notes. Natural simply means it is a regular note. However, there are five other notes that are usually placed in-between these natural notes. This brings the total number of notes in the music alphabet to 12. These five other notes are represented as *sharp notes* (♯) and *flat notes* (♭).

A sharp note is a note that is higher in pitch than its natural letter. For example, G♯ (pronounced G sharp) is higher than G. On the other hand, a flat note is a note lower than its natural letter, so A♭ (pronounced A flat) is lower in pitch than A. These sharp and flat notes are used to represent the black keys on a keyboard.

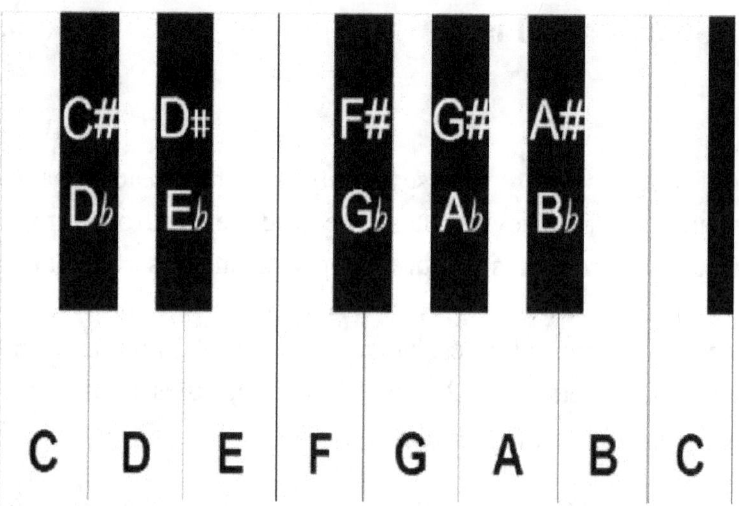

Figure 3.2

From the image above, you can see that in some instances, the sharps and flats occupy the same key. This means that they refer to the same note but are given different names depending on where they are used. This is what is known as ***enharmonics***. In other words, F♯ is the same note as Gb, and C♯ is the same note as Db, and so on.

If you are keen, you may have noticed that there are some notes that do not have any sharps or flats between them. This happens between the E-F notes and B-C notes. This shouldn't be taken to mean that there is no E♯ or Cb. We simply refer to them as F or B. So, when you raise an E by one note you get an F. Also, when you lower a C note you get a B.

The sharp symbol usually indicates that the particular note is one half-step higher than its natural equivalent. For example, G♯ is one half-step higher than G. In the same way, the flat symbol indicates that the note is one half-step lower than its natural equivalent. So, A♭ is one half-step lower than A.

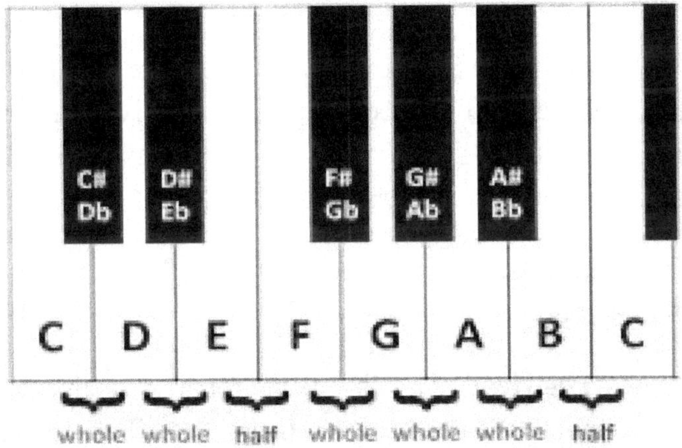

Figure 3.3

In other words, the distance between the G note and the A note is **one whole step**. When you see two adjacent notes having a sharp or a flat note between them, then that means that they are a whole step apart. Therefore, from figure 3.3, it is clear to see that most of the notes on the keyboard are one whole step apart except the E-F notes and B-C notes. These are only one half-step apart.

Parts of a Note

In common notation, sounds are written in form of notes. The two most critical pieces of information that written music should convey to a musician are the pitch to be played and its duration. A note that is placed high on the staff should be played at a higher sound.

To determine the pitch of a note, look at the clef, key signature, and the line or space the note is placed. To determine the duration of a note (how long it lasts), you look at the shape of the note, its tempo, and time signature.

There are three specific parts of a note. There is the head, the stem, and the flag.

- **The Head** (3) – This is the rounded section of a note. The head can be shaded or hollow. Every note must have a head.

- **The Stem** (2) – This is the vertical straight line that is linked to the head. Quavers, crotchets and minims all contain stems. Stems can point either up or down depending on the position of the note on the staff. Notes on or above the centre line have stems pointing down. Notes below the centre line have stems pointing up.

- **The Flag** (1) – This is the line that sticks out from the top or bottom of the stem. Only quavers and shorter notes carry flags.

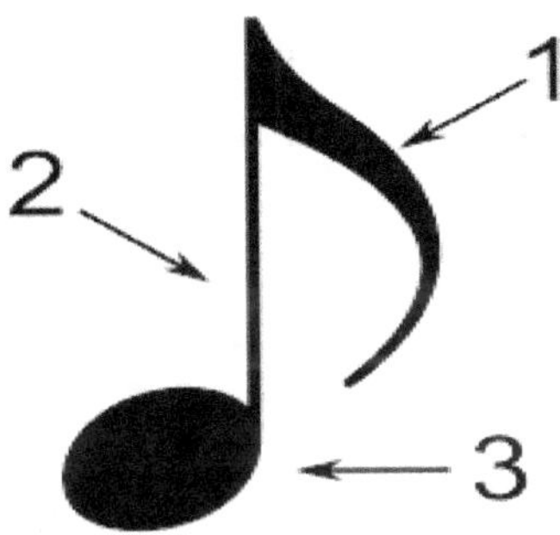

Figure 3.4

The pitch of a note is determined by the position of the head of the note, not the entire body. The head, the stem and the flag are all factors that must be considered when deciding how much time a note is given.

Note Duration and Values

Note duration is defined as the amount of time that a note is played. Each note usually has its own value, and these include the semibreve, minim, crotchet, quaver, and semiquaver. They are shown in this exact order in the image below.

Figure 3.5

The Whole (Semibreve) Note

This note is represented by a hollow oval and has no stem. It is the longest note in modern music and lasts for a full four beats.

This means that for four entire beats, all you must do is play and hold that one note.

The Half (Minim) Note

This is half the value of a semibreve and is held for half as long as the whole note. Two minims occupy the same length of time as a semibreve. It is represented by a hollow oval with a stem.

The Quarter (Crotchet) Note

This is a quarter of a semibreve. Four crotchets occupy the same length of time as a semibreve, which means a crotchet is one beat long. It is represented by a shaded oval with a stem.

The Eighth (Quaver) Note

This is half the length of time as a crotchet. It is represented by a shaded oval with a stem and a flag. The flag cuts the value of a note by half.

The Sixteenth (Semiquaver) Note

Two semiquavers occupy the same length of time as one quaver. It is represented by a shaded oval with a stem and two flags.

If two notes that have flags are next to each other, they are sometimes connected using a *beam*. This makes it possible to group flagged notes so that the music is easier and faster to read. The same principle also applies to semiquavers. A note must have the same number of beams as it does flags.

Figure 3.6: Semiquaver with beam

Dotted Notes

By now you know that a minim is half the length of a semibreve; a crotchet is half of a minim, and so on. But what do you do if you want a note length that is not half of another note? That's where the dotted note comes in. A dotted note is 1 ½ times the length of the same note. So, you end up with the original note length and half of that note length. For example, a dotted minim would have a duration that is as long as a minim plus a crotchet; or three crotchets.

If a note has two dots, it simply means that each dot adds half the length of the previous note. This is shown in figure 3.7 below.

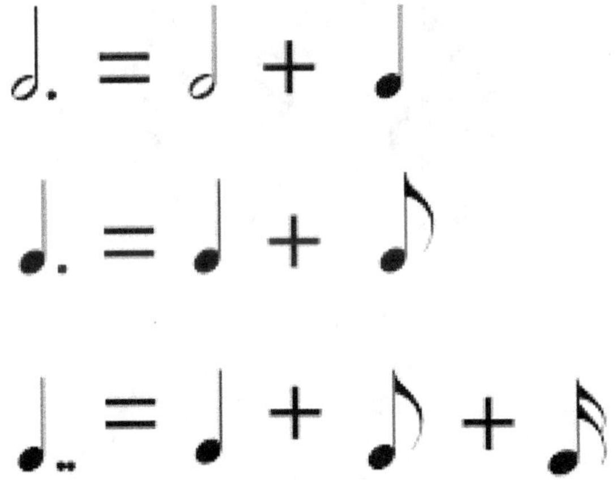

Figure 3.7

Time Signatures

These are usually indicated at the front end of the staff and are placed after the clef symbol and key signature. The time signature doesn't appear on every staff. It is used only when there is a change in the meter. *Meter* refers to the basic rhythm of the music. Time signature represents the meter and tells you how you should write it.

A fraction represents time signatures. The number at the top indicates the number of beats per measure while the number at the bottom indicates the type of note that will be used to carry the beat. The next section explains this more clearly.

Figure 3.7

Beats

There are many ways to organize music, and one of them is by splitting the time into small periods known as *beats*. Most of the actions that go with a piece of music occur at the start of the beat. For example, when you tap your foot or clap your hands, you are making those sounds or movements at the start of the beat. This is usually referred to as being "on the downbeat" since it corresponds to the moment when the conductor's baton reaches the bottom of its path.

The downbeat is the most substantial section of a beat, though some are stronger than the rest. Beats form a pattern such as strong-weak-weak-strong-weak-weak. Therefore, beats are further grouped into measures or bars. For example, a beat such as strong-weak-weak-strong-weak-weak would be written as 1-2-3-1-2-3, which means that each measure must contain three beats.

We already talked about how time signature indicates the number of beats per measure and the kind of note that carries a beat. For example, figure 3.7 has a time signature that requires three quarter (crotchet) notes in all the measures on that particular staff. In other words, every measure will have three crotchets. We usually say that such a piece is in "three four" time.

Don't forget what we learned earlier. A crotchet (quarter) note is one beat long. In other words, every measure on the staff should have the equivalent of three beats. These can still be represented as one minim and a crotchet, or six quavers per measure.

Exercise 2

1. Complete the following series of natural notes: A B
    _ _ E F _ _

2. Provide an alternative name for the following:

    a. A♯

    b. D♭

    c. G♭

    d. E♭

Fill in the blanks:

3. 1 semibreve = ___________ quavers

4. 1 minim = ___________ quarters

5. 1 minim = 1 quarter + ___________ eighths

6. Draw two staves with a treble clef symbol and time
    signatures showing *two four-time, three eight time,*
    and *six four time*. Fill in each measure with a
    different combination of note lengths. Use at least
    one dotted note in each staff.

Chapter Summary

Here are some of the key points you need to remember:

- A note is a letter that represents the pitch made by a musical instrument.
- An octave is a set of notes from one letter to the next pitch by the same letter name.
- The symbol ♯ represents sharp notes.
- Flat notes are represented by the symbol♭.
- Enharmonics are two notes that have equal pitches but are known by different names.
- There are five note values - semibreve, minim, quarter, quaver, and semiquaver. Each note lasts half the beat of the previous one.
- Music is divided into short time periods called beats.
- The time signature is shown using a fraction. The number at the top indicates the number of beats per measure. The number at the bottom indicates the type of note that will be used to carry the beat.

In the next chapter, you will learn about the building blocks of music. These are the basic elements of every musical piece, and they include aspects like rhythm, harmony, melody, timbre, and dynamics.

Chapter Four: The Basic Elements Music

In this chapter, you will learn about the essential elements that make music what it really is. These are aspects that even non-musicians can understand. As long as you have an appreciation for good music, you should be able to pick out these musical building blocks.

We are going to cover a number of these basic elements here. It is also important to note that musical theory experts hold differing opinions as to the total number of the elements of music. Some claim that there are as few as four while others say that there are as many as 10. Here we shall be covering rhythm, harmony, melody, timbre, texture, and dynamics.

Creating Rhythm

The primary reason why we study music theory is to be able to describe different musical pieces regarding how similar or different they are about the above six elements. Rhythm is considered one of the most basic components of any kind of music. Some types of music don't have harmony or melody, but every piece of music must have rhythm.

So, what exactly is rhythm?

Rhythm can be defined as the pattern of sounds repeated throughout the music. We can also say that rhythm is the arrangement of note lengths in music. Music and time go hand in hand, which means that rhythm has to be heard over a period of time. Rhythm is usually shaped by the meter and incorporates other elements such as *tempo* and *beat*.

Tempo is the speed at which you play a particular piece of music. When creating a composition, you indicate the tempo using an Italian word. For example, if you look at the starting point of a score, you may see words like *Largo* (slow pace), *Moderato* (moderate pace), or *Presto* (very fast pace). Here are some common tempo markings and their translations:

- Adagio – slow

- Vivo – lively and brisk

- Lento – slow

- Molto – a lot

- Mosso – motion or movement

- Piu – more

- Allegro – fast

- (un) poco – a little

- Meno – less

Harmony

Harmony is the result of having more than one pitch being heard at the same time. When you hear two or more notes being played at one time, you are listening to harmony. Harmony provides support for the melody and gives it texture. Harmony is usually described as being diminished, augmented, major, and minor.

Melody

Melody can be described as the general tune that is created when you play a succession of notes. It is influenced by your rhythm and pitch. A musical piece can have just one melody running through it, or it may have several melodies stacked in a verse-chorus form.

Timbre

Timbre is the quality of a sound that differentiates one musical instrument or voice from another. It is also called *tone color*. Timbre has nothing to do with the volume, length, or pitch of a sound.

For example, if you play a specific note on a clarinet and then on an oboe for five seconds at a specific volume, a listener can easily know that the notes are different. This is because the timbre of a clarinet is different from that of an oboe.

Texture

This refers to the type and number of layers that are used in a musical composition. Texture can be a single melodic line (monophonic), several melodic lines (polyphonic), or the main melody together with chords (homophonic).

Dynamics

This is the intensity that a musical piece is performed. In written music, dynamics are represented by symbols or abbreviations that indicate the volume that a note should be sung or played. Just like tempo, dynamics are derived from Italian words. For example, *fortissimo* indicates an extremely loud passage while *pianissimo* indicates an extremely soft section of music.

Here are some typical dynamic markings:

- mf mezzo forte   = medium loud

- f forte   = loud

- ff fortissimo   = very loud

- fff fortississimo = very, very loud

- p piano   = soft

- pp pianissimo   = very soft

- mp mezzo piano = medium soft

Exercise 3

1. Test yourself and see whether you can interpret what these Italian tempo markings mean:

   - Poco pin mosso

   - Piu vivo

   - Un poco allegro

   - Molto adagio

2. Write these dynamics in order from the quietest to the loudest: f, p, mf, ff, pp, and mp

Chapter Summary

Here are some of the key points you need to remember:

- Rhythm is the pattern of sounds repeated throughout the music.
- Rhythm depends on the tempo and beat of the music
- Tempo refers to the pace of the music and is usually indicated by Italian words.
- Harmony is created when more than one pitch is played at the same time.
- Melody is the general tune created when a succession of notes is played. A musical piece can have one or more melodies.
- Timbre is what tells us the difference between sounds made by different instruments.
- Texture is the number and type of layers in a musical composition. It can be monophonic, polyphonic, or homophonic.
- Dynamics is the intensity that music is played, and its markings are derived from Italian words.

In the next chapter, you will learn more about the different types of music scales. These are considered to be subsets of the notes you learned in Chapter 3.

Chapter Five: Forming Music Scales

In this chapter, you will learn how to create the different types of music scales. You will start with the simplest one, which is the major scale, and then proceed onto the more complex minor scale.

Music scales can be described as a set of notes arranged in sequential order, chosen to be used for a particular song. Why do we choose those notes? Simply because they sound great together! Though different cultures have adopted a variety of scales, the most common one is the major scale.

In order to create a scale, you need to go through the music alphabet (remember the seven letters from A to G?) and pick out notes that go well together. The notes chosen must achieve a particular sound. In most cases, you can do this by combining whole steps and half steps.

Tonal Centre

Every scale begins with the note that it is named after. That particular note is referred to as the ***tonal centre*** of that scale, and it is where the music in that scale feels "at rest."

For example, in most cases, music in the C major scale always ends on a C major chord. The music will begin on the C note, return to the C note repeatedly, and the melody will be based on the C note so much that listeners be able to identify where the tonal centre of that piece of music is.

Major Scales

If you have ever heard a song that sounds cheerful, uplifting, and fun, then it was probably written in a major key. Music that is written using a particular key only uses some of the many notes available. This sequence of notes then forms what we call a scale. Major keys are used to build major chords to then form a major scale.

It is important to know that different songs can use different scales, and different parts of a song can also make use of different scales. Scales are normally written in a sequential order from one note to the next note of the same letter. For example, we can have a scale that ranges from note C to the next note C, as shown below.

C D E F G A B C

As we already learned, each set of seven letters of the music alphabet forms an octave. Therefore, we can say that the above scale is a one-octave scale. To create a two-octave scale, you simply continue the same sequence until you land on the next note with the same letter name.

C D E F G A B C D E F G A B C

The range of notes from C to C is what forms the scale for C major. None of the notes in this particular scale has a sharp or a flat. On the other hand, the D major scale has two sharps. These are F sharp and C sharp.

D E F♯ G A B C♯ D

So, the question you are probably asking is: How are we supposed to know which notes should be sharpened and which ones should be flattened? The first method involves the use of a chart. However, this can be a cumbersome way since you have to keep referring all the time. You may even be forced to cram all that information into your head. The better alternative is to learn how to use whole and half steps.

Whole Steps and Half Steps

We talked about how the pitch of a sound represents how high or low the sound is. In music, we usually say that one note is either much higher or lower than another. This distance between two pitches is known as a half step. If you look at figure 5.1 below, you will be able to understand this better. This method of counting up whole and half steps can be used to form music scales from scratch.

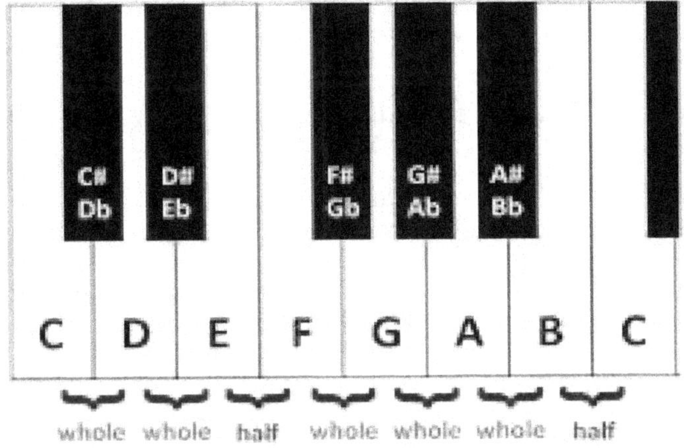

Figure 5.1

For example, we know that the distance from A to A♯ is a half step. The distance between B and B♭ is a half step. In other words, two consecutive half steps form a whole step. The format of any major scale usually follows this kind of sequence:

whole whole half whole whole whole half

This can also be written as:

w w h w w w h

This sequence means that there is a whole step between the first and second note, the second and third note, the fourth and fifth note, the fifth and sixth note, and the sixth and seventh note. There is a half step between the third and fourth note and the seventh and eighth note.

Please memorize this pattern because every major scale you encounter from here onwards will use this same sequence.

So, if we want to form the C major scale, we can write it as:

C w D w E h F w G w A w B h C

Figure 5.2

However, if we want to form the D major scale, we can write it as:

D w E w F# h G w A w B w C# h D

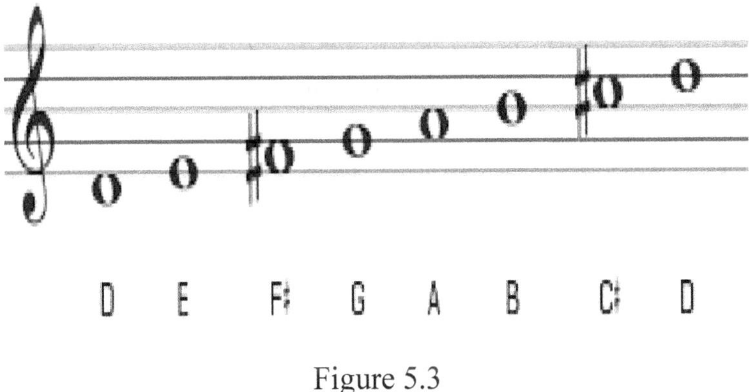

Figure 5.3

Minor Scales

Most people think of minor scales as confusing. This is because many music students usually start learning about the major scale first and end up focusing on it more than the minor scale. This situation isn't helped by the fact that there are a number of different types of minor scales that are often confused with one another. However, we will only focus on the most common minor scale in this book.

It is important to note that a piece of music in a particular major scale will sound the same as music in another major scale. For example, music that is in C major will sound somewhat similar to music in D major.

However, music in D major will sound very different from that in D minor because the notes in a minor scale are arranged in a very different pattern. Music written using a minor key has a sad, ominous, or mysterious sound than that written using a major key.

Natural Minor Scale

A natural minor scale is a scale where every note is played in a minor key signature. A natural minor scale is formed by starting at the tonal centre and moving upward using the following step pattern:

Whole half whole whole half whole whole

w h w w h w w

For example, music written in D minor scale will look like this:

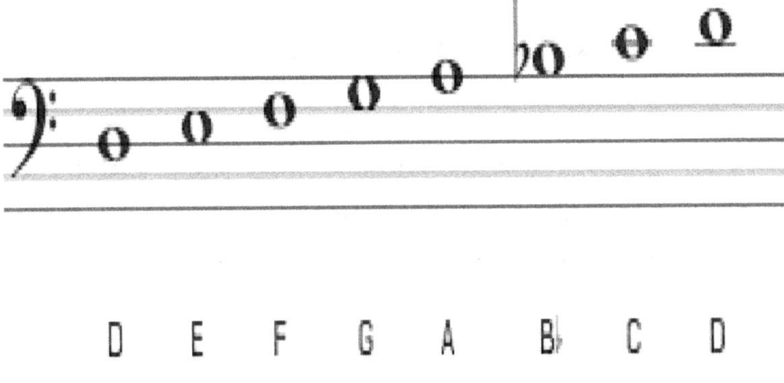

Figure 5.4

Exercise 4

1. Draw a staff with a treble clef. Write down the notes of the A major scale.

2. Draw a staff with a bass clef. Write down the notes of the G flat major scale.

3. Draw a staff with a treble clef. Write down the notes of the F minor scale.

4. Draw a staff with a treble clef. Write down the notes of the A flat minor scale.

Chapter Summary

Here are the key points to remember from this chapter:

- A music scale is a set of notes that sound good together, arranged in sequential order, within a particular piece of music.
- The tonal centre is the first note in a scale and is used to name that particular scale.
- To remember the sequence of notes in a major scale, follow the pattern *w w h w w w h*.
- A natural minor scale is written in a minor key and follows the pattern *w h w w h w w*.

In the next chapter, you will learn about the different types of intervals and how they are built.

Chapter Six: Building Intervals

In this chapter, you will learn about the different types of intervals and how to name them. Intervals are a very important concept in music. In fact, you cannot learn about scales or chords without making some reference to intervals. As a serious student of music theory, you must take the time to learn intervals and how to identify them.

Defining Intervals

An interval can be defined as the distance or space between two notes or pitches. Intervals are described using whole steps and half steps, which we have already covered in the previous chapters. The uncomplicated way to describe an interval would be to say, "E natural is one-half step below F natural," or "A flat is one step and a half away from F."

However, these are small distances. What about when we need to describe longer intervals in a major or minor scale?

How to Name Intervals

The primary factor you have to consider when naming an interval is the distance between the two notes. You need to look at how the notes are presented and then count the spaces and lines between the notes in the staff. Make sure that you include the spaces or lines that the notes are positioned on.

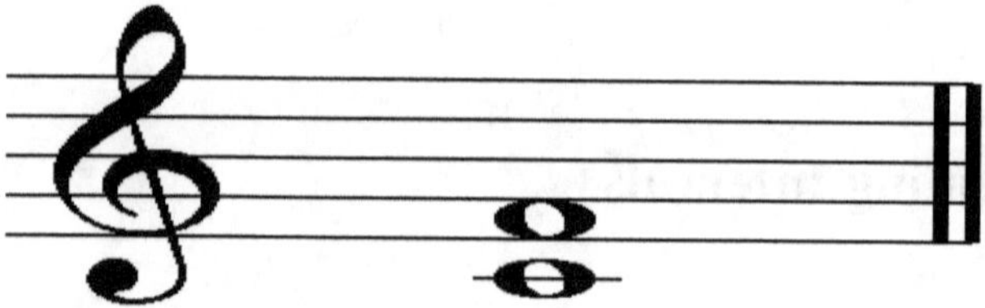

Figure 6.1

Figure 6.2

In figure 6.1 above, the interval between the C and F notes is four. We refer to this *a fourth*. In figure 6.2, the interval count between C and E is a third. At this point, the type of clef, key signature, and accidental (flats and sharps) don't matter.

If the interval between the notes is less or equal to one octave, it is referred to as a **simple interval** *(fig 6.3)*. If the interval is greater than one octave, it is called a **compound interval** *(fig 6.4)*.

Figure 6.3

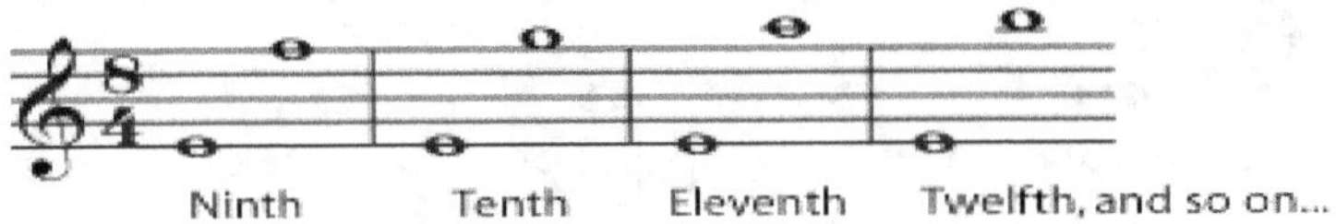

Figure 6.4

Now in the next phase of identifying an interval, we will consider the clef, key signature, and accidentals.

Perfect Intervals

Certain intervals are considered to be perfect intervals. They include primes, fourths, fifths, and octaves. They are called perfect because their sound waves are related very closely to one another. This makes these intervals sound good together.

Another name for a perfect prime is **unison,** which represents two notes that produce the same pitch. A perfect fourth has 5 half steps and a perfect fifth has 7 half steps. A perfect octave is where two notes are eight intervals apart, that is, 12 half steps apart. It is important that you understand how these steps are counted. You can go back and refresh your knowledge from the previous chapter on scales.

Figure 6.5

Major and Minor Intervals

The rest of the simple intervals form the major and minor intervals. These include seconds, thirds, sixths, and sevenths. A minor interval is one half-step smaller than a major one. They are described as follows:

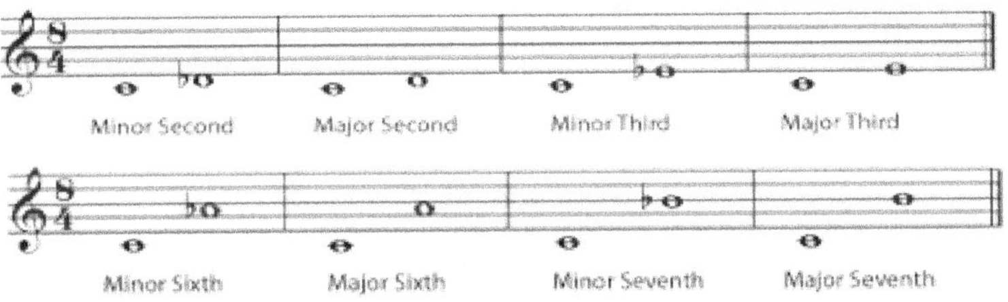

Figure 6.6

- Minor second – 1 half step

- Major second – 2 half steps

- Minor third – 3 half steps

- Major third – 4 half steps

- Minor sixth – 8 half steps

- Major sixth – 9 half steps

- Minor seventh – 10 half steps

Exercise 5

1. Give the complete name of the intervals.

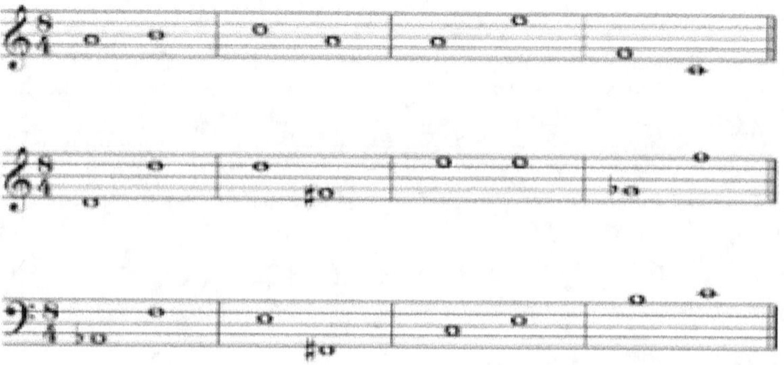

Chapter Summary

Here are the key points that you need to remember:

- Interval is the distance between two pitches.
- In order to name an interval, count the lines and spaces between the two notes. Don't forget to include the line or space the notes are standing on.
- The second phase of naming an interval must consider the half steps. The clef, key signature, and accidentals are important here.
- A simple interval is one octave or smaller, while a compound interval is greater than one octave.
- Intervals are considered perfect if their sound waves are closely related. Perfect intervals include primes, fourths, fifths, and octaves
- A perfect prime is also called unison.
- A minor interval is one half-step smaller than a major interval. These intervals include seconds, thirds, sixths, and sevenths.

In the next chapter, you will learn about key signatures and the circle of fifths.

Chapter Seven: Key Signatures

In this chapter, you will learn about how to use key signatures to make the performance of music much easier. You will also learn about the major and minor key signatures as well as how to read the circle of fifths.

Key signatures are a very important part of music. The key signature is what we use to know the pitches that a song will be performed. Every time that a piece of music is performed, it is played in a particular key or tonality. For example, if a song is to be played using the D key, then the entire song must be based around a D chord or a D note. Even the notes used will be from a D scale. The key signature represents all this information.

So how do we know the key that is being used?

If you look at the beginning of every line of written music, you will notice that there are sharps or flats (also known as accidentals) right after the clef symbol. These accidentals tell us the key to use. It is important to note that a key can either be a sharp or a flat, but it can never be both.

So, what is the significance of using keys? When you are writing a long piece of music in a single key, you will soon find it very tedious to keep repeating the accidentals all over the staff. Look at the image below to see what a simple melody in D major looks like if you don't use a key signature.

Figure 7.1

Now, this is just a short section of a piece of music. If you were writing a full song, the staff would get quite messy, not to mention the fact that you would get tired of writing all those sharps. So, to avoid this, music composers use key signatures only at the beginning of the staff to show the performers which pitches must have accidentals.

Below is the same simple melody in D major. But this time it has a key signature that indicates that the notes C and F should be sharpened.

Figure 7.2

The Circle of Fifths

This is a graphical way of arranging keys to show how closely related they are to each other. The circle of fifths has been part of music theory for centuries, and it provides a great method for summarizing the key signatures to be used for any key that has a maximum of seven sharps or flats.

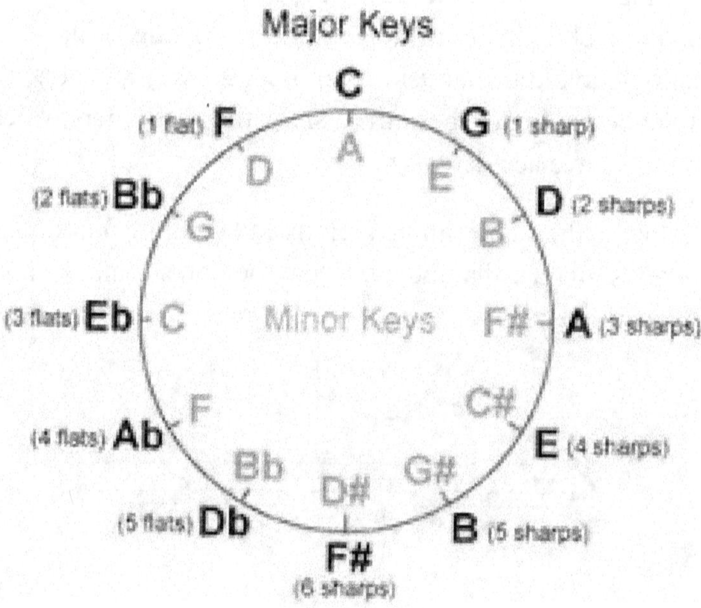

Figure 7.3

So how will you know which notes in the key are supposed to be sharpened or flattened? In order to use the circle of fifths to identify your key signature, you must use a mnemonic device to help you memorize the order of sharps and flats.

The first thing to do is memorize the order of notes on the following circle:

F C G D A E B

Most people use the mnemonic *Father Charles Goes Down And Ends Battle*

If you want to determine the sharp keys, you move clockwise around the circle of fifths. Then you read the mnemonic forward. For example, according to the circle of fifths, there are three sharps in the key A major. But which notes exactly are supposed to be sharp?

Moving clockwise along the circle and following the order of notes, you will identify the notes to be sharpened as F, C, and G.

If you want to determine the flat keys, you must move anticlockwise along the circle, and then read the mnemonic backward. For example, according to the circle of fifths, there are four flats in the key for A-flat major. But which notes should be flattened?

Moving anticlockwise along the circle and backward along the order of notes, you will see that B, E, A, and D are the notes that will have flats.

The reason why we call it a circle of fifths is because as you move from one section (or key) to the next, you are moving down or up by an interval of a perfect fifth. If you move clockwise by a perfect fifth, you will land on a key with one sharp more or one flat less than where you started. If you move anticlockwise a perfect fifth, you land on a key that has one flat more or one sharp less than where you started.

Minor Key Signatures

So far, we have been focusing more on the major keys. However, minor keys also have signatures. Every major key you see on the circle of fifths has a corresponding minor key with the exact same signature. Minor and major keys that have corresponding key signatures are referred to as *relative keys*. For example, both F major and D minor have one flat. F major is regarded as the relative major of D minor while D minor is regarded as the relative minor of F major.

In other words, just because keys are next to each other on a keyboard (the chromatic scale) does not mean that they are closely related. The main factor that determines the relationship is having similar key signatures. The closer the keys are in the circle of fifths, the closer their relationship in terms of key signature.

This means that the next most closely related keys to F major and D minor are C major (or A minor), and B major (or G minor). Those keys that don't correspond at all with the key signature of F major are on the opposite side of the circle.

Exercise 6

1. Which keys in the circle of fifths are closely related to F sharp major and B flat major?

2. Name the major and minor keys for each key signature.

Chapter Summary

Here are the key points to remember:

- Key signatures tell us the pitches that a song will be performed in.
- To make writing music much easier, the key signature is placed at the beginning of the staff instead of between the notes in the staff.
- The accidentals indicate the key to be used in a piece of music.
- The circle of fifths is a graphical illustration of keys and indicates how closely related they are to each other.
- To determine the key being used, look at the number of sharps or flats in the key signature.
- To identify key signatures, use the mnemonic Father Charles Goes Down And Ends Battle (FCGDAEB).
- To identify the sharp keys, move clockwise around the circle and read the mnemonic forwards.
- To identify the flat keys, move anticlockwise and read the mnemonic backward.
- Major and minor keys that have corresponding key signatures are known as relative keys.

In the next chapter, you will learn about triads, chords, and chord progressions.

Chapter Eight: Building Chords

In this chapter, you will learn chords, which are the building blocks of the tone of a piece of music. Learning how to build chords can be a bit challenging for beginners, but the trick lies in taking it one step at a time. For that reason, we are going to focus on building triads, major chords, and minor chords.

Chords

A chord is simply a group of notes that are played together. Most of the sad songs you hear use what are known as minor chords. The upbeat songs tend to use suspended second chords or major seventh chords. Chords can either be used to make melodies or they can be arranged in specific sequences known as progressions to create a sense of direction and movement in music.

Triads

Chords are a set of three or more pitches that are played together. A chord that is made up of three notes that can be arranged as thirds is known as a *triad*. The fastest way to know if a chord of three notes is a triad is to arrange the notes in a circle of thirds. If the pitch classes of the three notes sit next to each other, then they form a triad.

There are two ways of identifying a triad, i.e., according to its root and its quality. The ***root of chord,*** which is the note that gives the chord its name, is the lowest note. The second note in the triad is known as the ***third of chord***, while the last note in the triad is called the ***fifth of chord***. After you position the root of chord, you then place the third of chord a third higher than the root. The fifth of chord is then placed a fifth higher than the root, which coincides with a third higher than the third of chord. If you find this confusing, you may need to go to Chapter 6 (figure 6.3) where we learned about intervals.

In the figure below, the chord is written in the root position as a stack of third, which is the easiest way to write down a triad. Don't forget that in most cases, the root is the bottom note, unless you are dealing with an inversion.

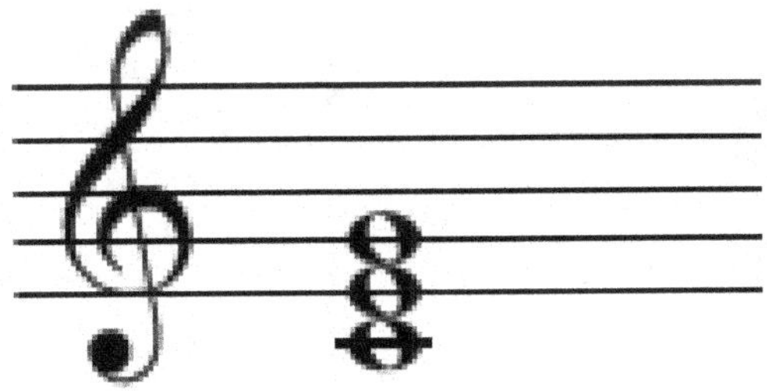

Figure 8.1

First and Second Inversions

First inversion occurs when the third of chord becomes the lowest note. In case the fifth of chord is placed at the bottom, then the chord is said to be in *second inversion*. The second inversion is also known as a *six-four chord* because the intervals are a sixth and a fourth.

The most important factor in a chord is not the distance between the top two notes from the lowest note. The number of notes also isn't an issue. The thing that matters the most is which note is at the bottom.

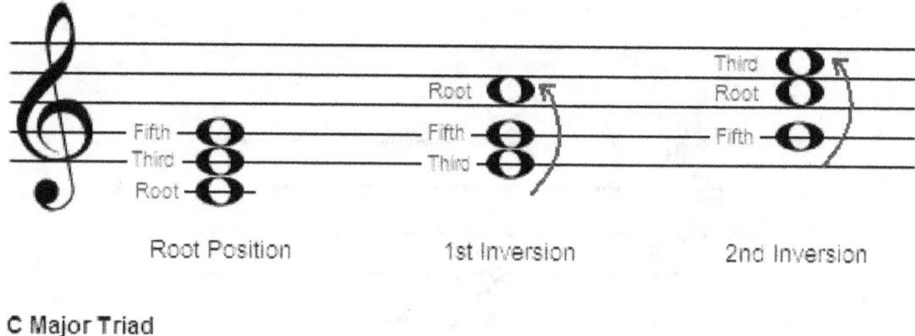

Figure 8.2

Triad Qualities

The first step in determining the quality of a triad is to identify the interval between the root and the other notes in the chord. The four qualities of triads that can be found in major and minor scales include:

- Major triad – M3 and P5 above root

- Minor triad – m3 and p5 above root

- Diminished triad – m3 and d5 above root

- Augmented triad – M3 and A5 above root

The two most common triads are the major and minor chords. In these two types of chords, the root of the chord and fifth of chord are at an interval of a perfect fifth, which are 7 half steps. This interval can be split into a major third, which is 4 half-steps, and a minor third, which forms 3 half-steps.

A ***major chord*** is formed when the major third falls between the root and the third of chord. A ***minor chord*** is formed when the minor third falls between the root and the third of chord.

On the other hand, diminished and augmented chords do not have a perfect fifth, which explains why they produce an anxious feeling in listeners. **Augmented chords** are formed when two major thirds are combined, thus creating an augmented fifth. **Diminished chords** are formed when two minor thirds are combined, thus creating a diminished fifth.

Figure 8.3

Seventh Chords

This is a chord that is formed when you take a triad and combine it with a note that is a seventh above the root. There are many different varieties of seventh chords, and we distinguish them according to the type of seventh and type of triad used. Here are some of the most common types of seventh chords:

- Dominant seventh chord – This is a combination of a major triad and a minor seventh

- Minor seventh chord – This is a combination of a minor triad and a minor seventh

- Major seventh chord – This is a combination of a major triad and a major seventh

- Diminished seventh chord – This is a combination of a diminished triad and a diminished seventh

- Half-diminished seventh chord – This is a combination of a diminished triad and a minor seventh

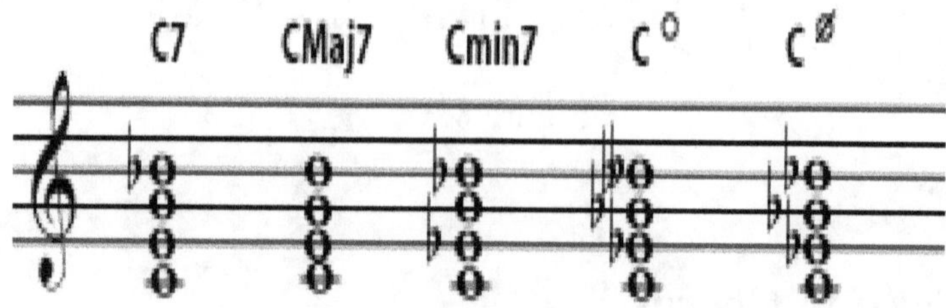

Figure 8.4

Exercise 7

1. Write these seventh chords – G minor seventh; B flat
   major seventh; F sharp minor seventh; and D
   diminished seventh.

Chapter Summary

Here are some of the key points that you need to remember:

- A chord is a group of notes that are played together.
- A chord that comprises three notes arranged as
  thirds is known as a triad.
- Its root and quality can identify a triad.
- In a triad, the lowest note is the root of chord; the
  second note is the third of chord, and the last note is
  the fifth of chord.
- First inversion occurs when the third of chord
  becomes the lowest note.
- Second inversion occurs when the fifth of chord
  becomes the lowest note.
- When the interval between the root and third of
  chord is the major third, a major chord is formed.
- When the interval between the root and third of
  chord is the minor third, a major chord is formed.

- When two major thirds are combined, an augmented chord is formed.
- When two minor thirds are combined, a diminished chord is formed.
- A seventh chord is formed when you add a triad and a note that is a seventh above the root.

Final Words

You have come to the end of the book. Though it was a long journey, I'm sure you now have a much better understanding of music theory than before. If you had never studied the subject previously, you should be ready to move on to the more complex theories of music. If you already had a background in music, then your knowledge of music theory will help you become an even better musician. For those who were seeking a refresher course in some of the elements you had forgotten, consider your mind refreshed.

Music theory is not really as hard as it looks or sounds. The bottom line is that you have to have a solid foundation that will always be there to guide you. The seven elements of music we have covered in this book are the keys to unlocking any musical composition. On top of that, there are seven good exercises in this book that will help you crystallize the knowledge you have gained in each chapter.

The questions provided in every exercise have covered the fundamentals that every music student and musician must know like the back of their hand. If you were keen when reading the book, I'm sure you had an easy time answering them. If you felt like you were struggling a little bit, then don't worry about it. Just go back to the chapter where you feel uncertain and reread it. Some of the concepts usually take time to sink in. Don't forget that the answers to every question are on the last page of the book.

Being able to read and write music is a very rewarding experience, and now you are ready to move onto the next phase of your musical journey. Yes, that was the easy part. Anybody can buy a book, read it, and toss it aside. All it will cost you is some time and money. However, you must now do the hard work necessary to integrate and incorporate this new knowledge into your music. This book has provided you with an opportunity to learn something that can help you going forward. Don't stop here. What is important is that you continue to practice and challenge yourself. Never stop learning and always make an effort to put into practice everything that you have learned in this book.

I am honoured that you took the time to read this book. It was a pleasure for me to walk with you through your musical journey. I hope you enjoyed reading and learning from this beginner's guide to music theory.

Thank you and good luck!

Solutions to Exercise Questions

Solutions to Exercise 1

1. Draw the staff on a piece of paper and practice writing the two clef symbols on the staff. Draw as many as you can until you learn it perfectly.

2. Draw the staff with a treble clef and name all the spaces on the staff.

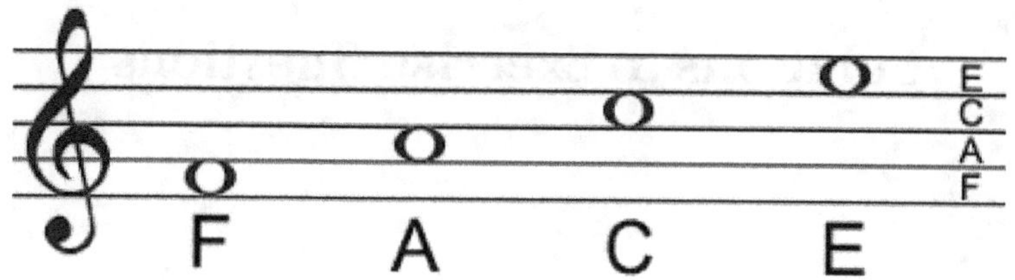

3. Draw the staff with a bass clef and name all the lines on it.

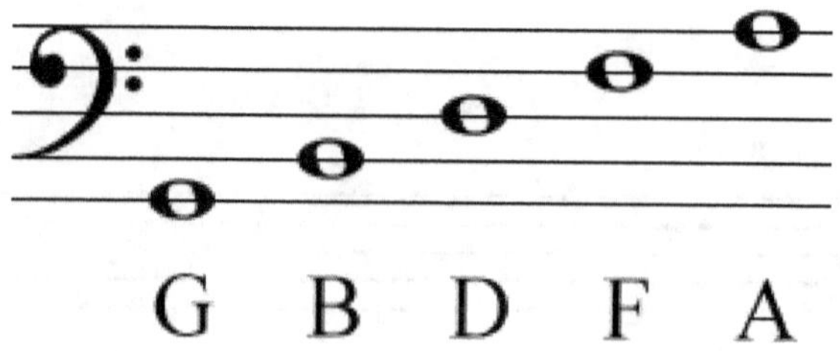

4. On a staff with a treble clef, name the ledger lines and spaces above the staff.

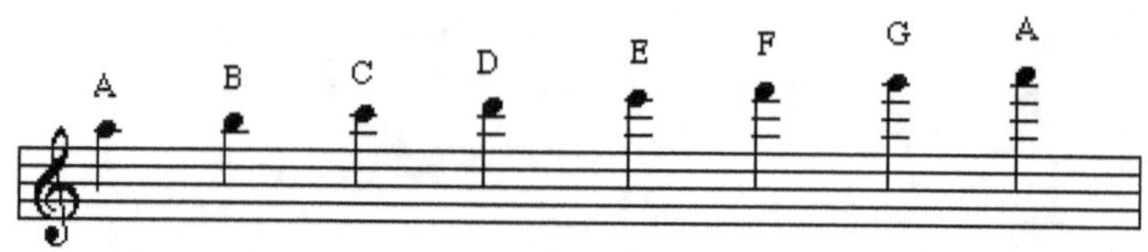

5. On a staff with a bass clef, name the ledger lines and
   spaces below the staff.

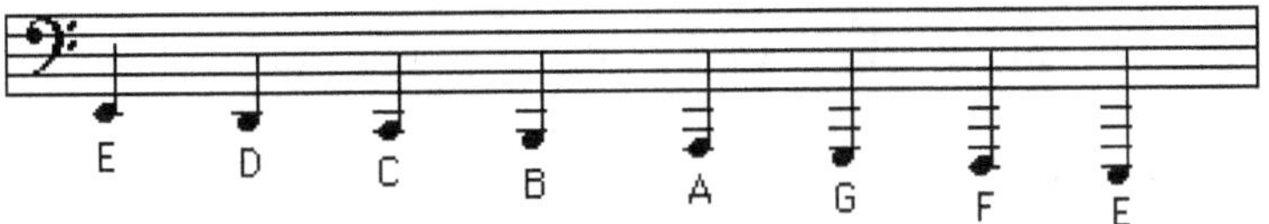

Solutions to Exercise 2

1. Complete the following series of natural notes: A B C D E F G A

2. Provide an alternative name for the following:

A♯ - B ♭

D♭ - C♯

G♭ - F♯

E♭ - D♯

3. 1 semibreve = 8 quavers

4. 1 minim = 4 quarters

5. 1 minim = 1 quarter + 2 eighths

6. Three staves with a treble clef symbol and time signatures showing *two four time*, *three eight time,* and *six four time*. Fill in each measure with a different combination of note lengths. Use at least one dotted note per staff.

Solutions to Exercise 3

1. Italian tempo markings:

   - Poco piu mosso – a little more movement/motion

   - Piu vivo – more lively

   - Un poco allegro – a little fast

   - Molto adagio – very slow

2. In order from quietest to loudest: pp, mp, p, f, mf, ff

Solutions to Exercise 4

1. The staff with a treble clef and notes of the A major scale.

2. The staff with a bass clef and notes of the G flat major scale.

G-flat major scale

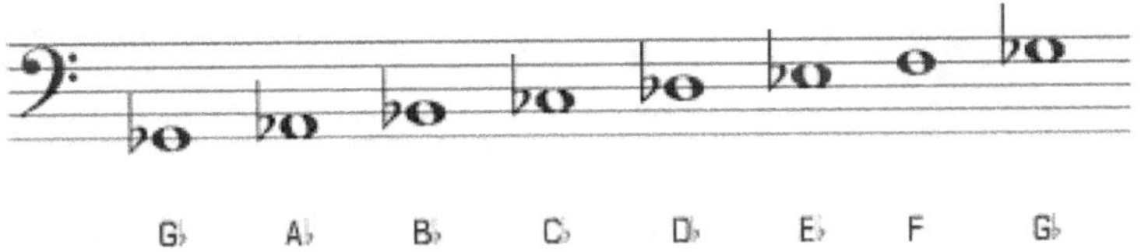

3. The staff with a treble clef and notes of the F minor scale.

F minor scale

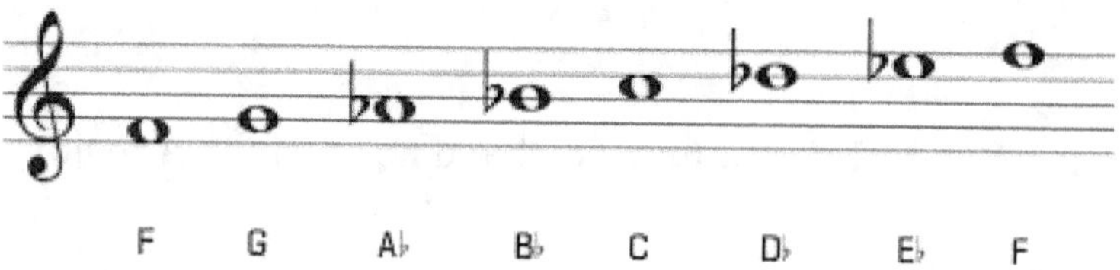

4. The staff with a treble clef and notes of the A flat minor scale.

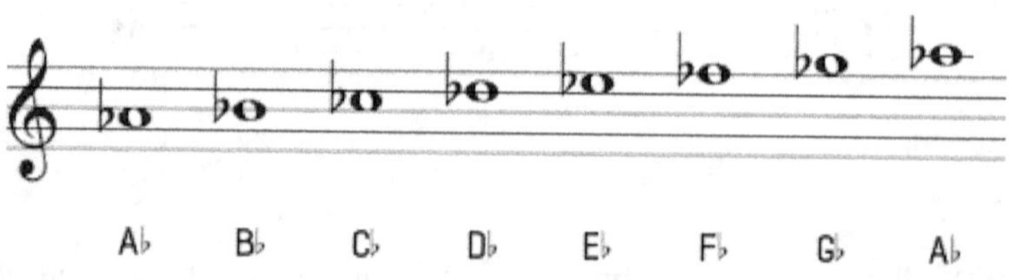

Solutions to Exercise 5

Names of intervals:

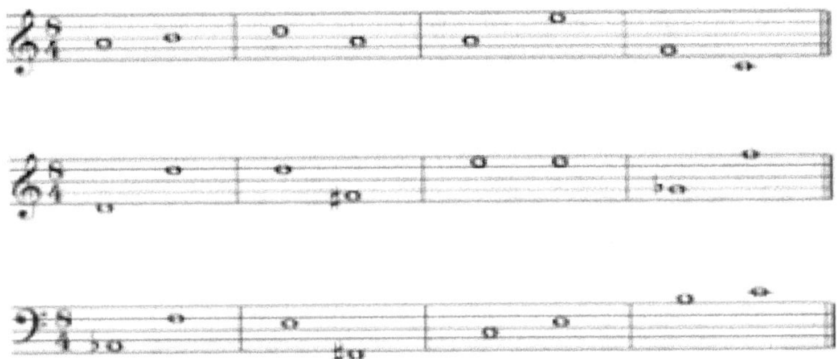

Top Staff:

Major Second - Minor Third - Perfect Fifth - Perfect Fourth

Centre Staff:

Perfect Octave – Minor Sixth – Perfect Prime (Unison) –
Major Seventh

Bottom Staff:

Major Sixth – Minor Seventh – Major Third – Minor
Second

Solution to Exercise 6

1. Relative keys to:

F sharp major – D sharp minor

B flat major – G minor

2. Major and minor keys for each key signature:

G Major – D Major – A Major – E Major

Solutions to Exercise 7

G minor 7th chord

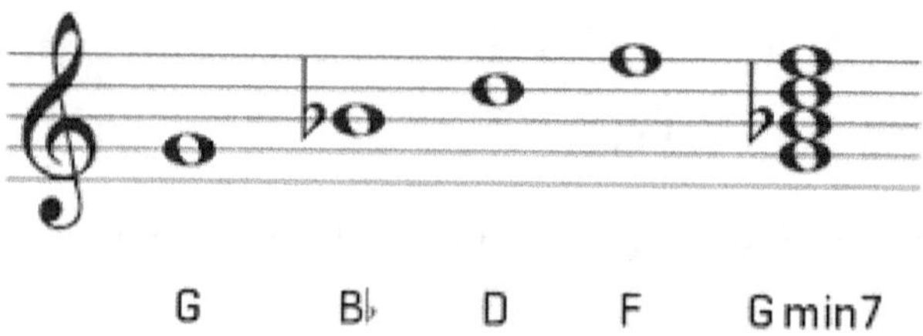

B-flat major 7th chord

F-sharp minor 7th chord

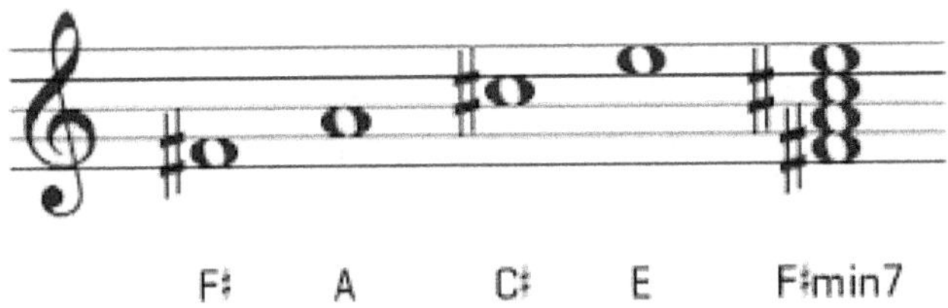

D diminished 7th chord

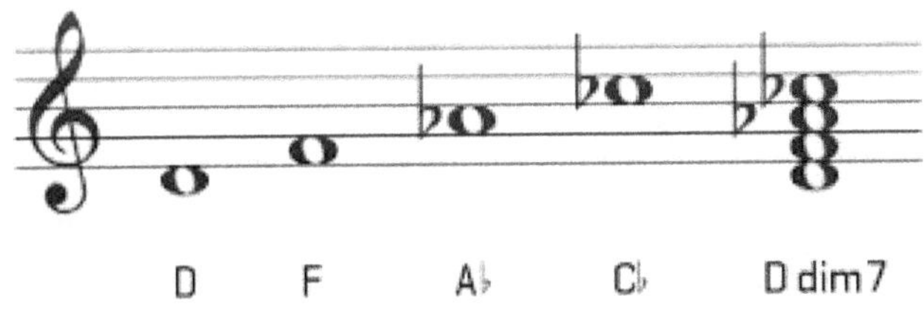